DATE DUE

APR 0 2 1992		

DEMCO 38-296

**WOODBRIDGE/ELEMENTARY
SCHOOL LIBRARY
ZEELAND PUBLIC SCHOOLS**

WATERGATE

WATERGATE

Scott Westerfeld

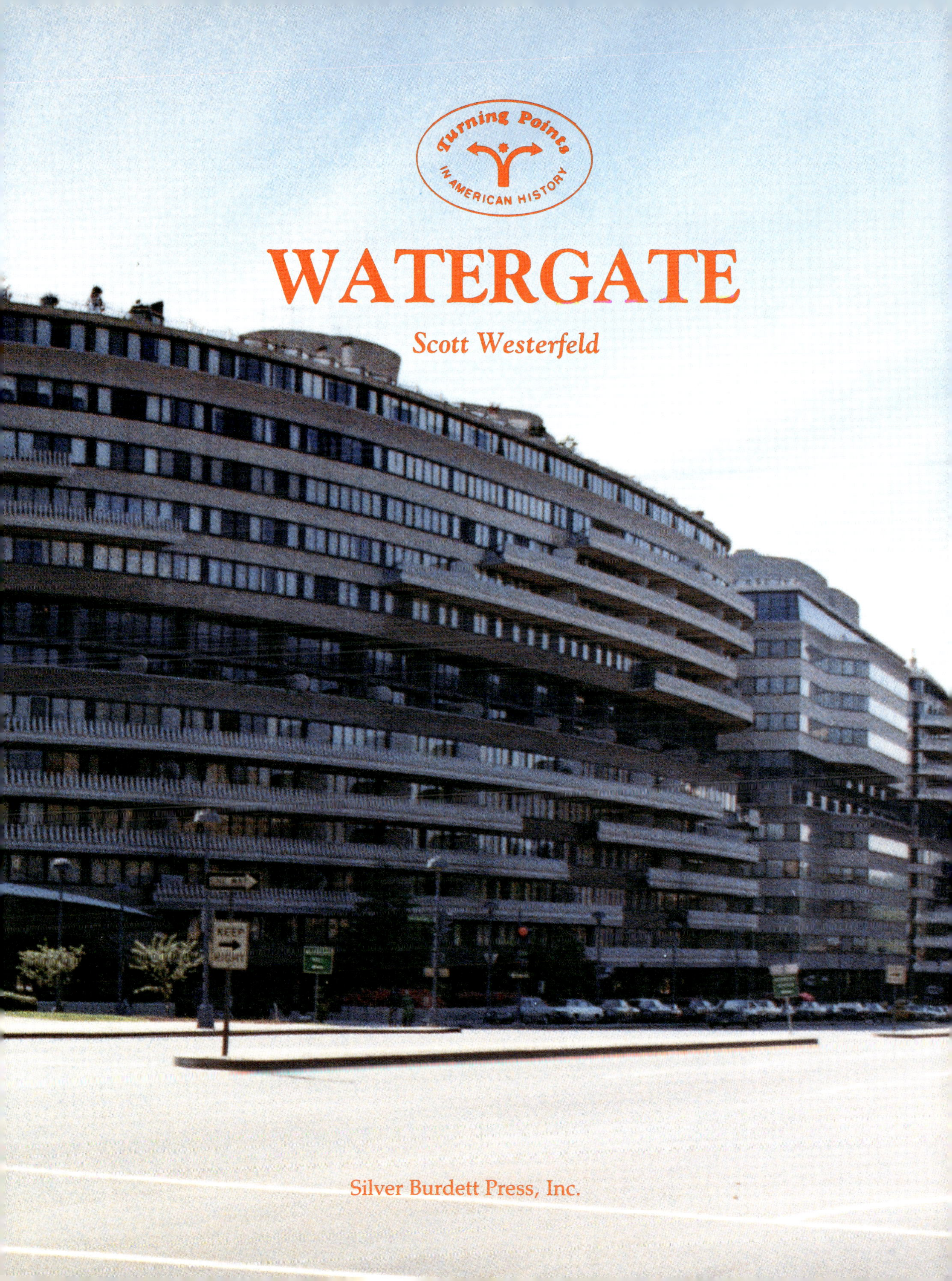

Silver Burdett Press, Inc.

Acknowledgments

The author and editor thank Tina Angelos and Nat Andriani of Wide World Photos for their invaluable help in text and picture research.

Consultants

Elizabeth Blackmar
Assistant Professor
Department of History
Columbia College
New York, New York

Robert M. Goldberg
Consultant to the Social Studies Department
 (formerly Department Chair)
Oceanside Middle School
Oceanside, New York

Cover: President Nixon speaking on television on April 29, 1974. Behind him are bound transcripts of the famous Watergate tapes. National Archives.

Title Page: The Watergate office-apartment complex in Washington, D.C., Wide World Photos.

Contents Page: A Nixon button from the 1960 presidential campaign. Private Collection.

Back Cover: The Senate Select Committee on Watergate listens to testimony. Wide World Photos.

Library of Congress Cataloging-in-Publication Data

Westerfeld, Scott.
    Watergate / Scott Westerfeld
       p. cm — (Turning points in American history)
    Includes bibliographical references and index.
    Summary: Analyzes events in the scandal known as Watergate, which paralyzed American politics and led to the downfall of President Richard Nixon.
      1. Watergate Affair, 1972-1974—Juvenile literature.
    [1. Watergate Affair, 1972-1974.]   I. Title. II. Series.
    E860.W47   1991
    364. 1' 32 ' 0973—dc20   91-7454
                                                        CIP
                                                          AC

Editorial Coordination by Richard G. Gallin

 Created by Media Projects Incorporated

Carter Smith, *Executive Editor*
Charles A. Wills, *Series Editor*
Bernard Schleifer, *Design Consultant*
Arlene Goldberg, *Cartographer*

Copyright © 1991 by Silver Burdett Press, Inc., a division of Simon & Schuster, Englewood Cliffs, New Jersey.

All rights reserved, including the right of reproduction in whole or part in any form.

Manufactured in the United States of America.

ISBN 0-382-24126-6 [lib. bdg.]
10 9 8 7 6 5 4 3 2 1

ISBN 0-382-24120-7 [pbk.]
10 9 8 7 6 5 4 3 2 1

CONTENTS

	Introduction "A THIRD-RATE BURGLARY"	7
1	THE RISE OF RICHARD NIXON	11
2	THE POWER OF THE PRESIDENT	25
3	"WHAT DID THE PRESIDENT KNOW?"	35
4	THE FALL OF A PRESIDENT	45
	Afterword A TIME OF HEALING	59
	Index	62
	Suggested Reading	64

INTRODUCTION

"A THIRD-RATE BURGLARY"

Frank Wills decided it was time to call the police.

For the second time that night, he had found the lock of a stairwell door taped open. It was 2:00 A.M., June 17, 1972. Wills believed that somewhere in the Watergate Hotel a burglary was taking place.

Wills worked as a night watchman at the Watergate, a hotel-office-apartment complex in Washington, D.C. The Watergate was an expensive residence, home to President Richard Nixon's personal secretary, Rose Mary Woods. The director of Nixon's campaign for reelection, former Attorney General John N. Mitchell, lived there, too.

The same hotel also housed the headquarters of the Democratic party's National Committee. It was an election year, and Democratic candidate George McGovern was running against Richard Nixon for the presidency.

The entrance to the Watergate complex.

When the police arrived, they discovered five burglars in the Democratic headquarters. The men surrendered to the police without a fight.

The five men carried some things that were unusual for ordinary burglars. The police found film, two cameras, and a large amount of cash in their possession. The burglars also had microphones for "bugging" telephones to secretly listen to conversations. The men gave false names to the police, but they carried papers that revealed their real identities. Four were Cuban Americans from Miami, and the fifth was named James W. McCord, Jr.

The next morning they were brought before Federal Judge James A. Belson. Four of them wouldn't give their occupations except to say they were "anti-Communists." James McCord said he was a security consultant who had recently retired from the Central Intelligence Agency.

By now the news of the break-in had

7

Police and telephone company technicians check the headquarters of the Democratic National Committee one day after the June 17, 1972, break-in.

spread. Reporters began trying to solve the mystery of the five burglars. Why had they broken into the Democratic headquarters? Where had their money come from? Who had hired them?

Before long, two clues came to light. One was that James McCord was indeed a security consultant, for the Committee to Re-elect the President. The other clue was that an address book found on one of the burglars contained the telephone number for E. Howard Hunt, a former member of the president's staff. Both clues pointed to the Nixon White House.

At first, the White House showed little concern with the break-in—at least publicly. The president's staff said they had nothing to do with it. White House press secretary Ronald Ziegler later called the Watergate break-in a "third-rate burglary."

The facts that emerged about the burglars, the money, and the president did not come quickly. In all, it would be two years before the painful story finally ended. The crisis that grew out of the attempted burglary would eventually engulf the attention of the entire nation. It would paralyze American politics and shatter many Americans' faith in their government for years.

At the time, however, there were only the burglars and a handful of clues. The answers behind the questions the break-in raised were concealed behind official silence, official lies, and the power of the president. The truth came slowly.

1

THE RISE OF RICHARD NIXON

When Richard Milhous Nixon entered politics, the United States was a nation happy to be at peace. In 1941, the nation had joined in the largest conflict in history, World War II. Now it was January 1946. The war had been won only a few months before. Everywhere, young men and women were returning from service overseas.

Richard Nixon spent the war as a naval officer in the Pacific. He hadn't even left the navy when he announced that he would run for the Congress of the United States. His red, white, and blue campaign posters, which showed him in his U.S. Navy uniform, said proudly, "Elect Richard M. Nixon—World War Two Veteran."

Nixon had little experience in politics. His only previous campaign had been for student body president at a small college in Whittier, California, the town where he had been born in 1913. The Nixon family didn't have much time for politics. His father owned a general store and gas station, but the business was never very successful. Richard Nixon, one of five children, had to help support the family by taking part-time jobs. Despite this hardship, he was an excellent student. After college, Nixon received a scholarship to study law at Duke University in North Carolina. He graduated in 1940 and married Thelma "Pat" Ryan that same year. The United States entered the war a year later.

The war was still fresh in Americans' minds when Nixon returned to Whittier to begin his campaign. He knew that many voters would welcome a war veteran. He also learned that the victory against Germany and Japan hadn't

Richard Nixon, with wife, Pat, and daughters, Julie and Patricia, on the way to the Republican National Convention in 1960.

Nixon (standing at center) with the Whittier College football team.

solved all the nation's problems. Many Americans feared the peace would not last. The Soviet Union, an ally during the war, was now seen as a new enemy.

The United States and the Soviet Union had put aside their differences to fight Nazi Germany together. But with Germany defeated, the United States was uneasy over the Soviet Union's actions. For example, Soviet troops remained in Eastern Europe, despite agreements made during the war.

Many people in the United States feared the Soviet Union because that nation hoped to spread Soviet-style communism throughout the world. The Soviet Union's ruthless dictator, Joseph Stalin, had ordered millions of people killed or imprisoned during his harsh rule. In the Soviet Union and the nations it controlled, basic human freedoms didn't exist. All power was concentrated in the hands of the Communist party.

Some Americans believed that a Communist conspiracy threatened to overturn freedom in the United States. For example, the wartime ties between Washington, D.C., and Moscow had led to dangerous secrets—like information about atomic weapons projects—reaching the Soviets. Between the threat of a Communist superpower abroad and the fear of Communists inside the United States, Richard Nixon found that a new war was beginning. This conflict became known as the cold war. It was a global conflict between the Soviet Union and the United States. Nuclear weapons made an actual war too dangerous to fight, so the cold war was fought indirectly; with spies and other secret warriors, and often with words. The fear the cold war created would serve Nixon's political career for years to come.

In the 1940s, politicians in California were known across the country for their fierce tactics. Campaign tactics often included spreading vicious rumors, publishing personal attacks on opponents, and using "dirty tricks." Nixon's first campaign, which used all these techniques, focused on a single issue: communism. Nixon and his supporters realized how easy it was to stir up strong emotions with that one word. They tried to convince voters that Nixon's opponent, Congressman Jerry Voorhis, was a tool of communism.

In that anxious time, Nixon's tough tactics worked. On election day, Nixon won by a landslide.

Congressman Richard Nixon soon gained national attention. One of his first assignments in Congress was to serve on the House Un-American Activities Committee. This committee was investigating charges that members of the U.S. State Department had given information about U.S. foreign policy to the Soviet Union. One of the officials charged was Alger Hiss, who had been

Nixon and Whittaker Chambers examine microfilmed documents during the Alger Hiss investigation, 1948.

Four views of Nixon during the "Checkers Speech" of 1952.

an aide to President Franklin Roosevelt. Whittaker Chambers, a journalist and former Communist, claimed that Hiss had passed State Department documents to the Soviets during World War II. Hiss denied the charges under oath.

Nixon discovered official documents hidden in a pumpkin on Whittaker Chambers's farm. These "pumpkin papers" appeared to have been typed on Hiss's typewriter. In a trial resulting from Nixon's efforts, Hiss was found guilty of perjury (lying under oath in court) and sentenced to prison.

With Hiss convicted, Nixon's fame grew. Some Americans, who believed Hiss was innocent, protested Nixon's tactics. But to many others, Nixon was a hero. In the 1948 congressional elections, Nixon easily won reelection.

In 1950, Nixon ran for a California Senate seat against Helen Gahagan Douglas. This campaign was even harsher than the race against Jerry Voorhis. Communism was an even bigger issue than before. Joseph McCarthy, a Republican senator from Wisconsin, had created a sensation by claiming he had a list of Communists in the federal government. With communism still in the public eye, Nixon again tried to portray his opponent as a tool of the Communists. In one case, he mailed voters a list of positions Douglas had taken in her career. The list was printed on red paper. The color suggested that she was a "red"—a Communist supporter. Because of these campaign tricks, Nixon became known as "Tricky Dick," a nickname he was never able to shake.

After this election ended in another victory for Nixon, Republicans began to see him as a national leader. In 1952, he was chosen to run for vice president in the presidential campaign of Dwight D. Eisenhower, the popular general who had led the Allies in World War II. Nixon was known for his fierce and successful campaigns. The Republicans had lost the last five presidential races, but now they felt they had a winning team.

The campaign went well at first. Before long, however, Nixon experienced his first political crisis. Reporters discovered that Nixon's supporters had raised a special fund to pay for his political expenses. Nixon claimed that the fund was legal and proper. Critics charged that the money seemed like a form of bribery. Newspapers fanned the fires of suspicion, and the leadership of the Republican party considered dropping Nixon from the race.

Nixon didn't panic. He decided to speak to the American people in a long televised appearance. In this speech, he said that he was not a wealthy man and could not afford to pay for his own political trips. As he often did in political speeches, Nixon spoke of the poverty he had known growing up. He finished by carefully detailing his finances, while reminding the audience that few politicians had ever revealed so much about their private lives. He admitted taking one gift from a supporter. The gift was a cocker spaniel named Checkers. The speech became famous as the "Checkers Speech."

The TV appearance was a huge success. It saved Nixon's political career and showed that he could handle a crisis. It also taught him the power of television, which was just becoming a part of politics. Eisenhower and Nixon went on to win the election.

As vice president, Nixon traveled all over the globe, gaining valuable experience by meeting many world leaders. Not all of his travels were pleasant. On a trip to Latin America in 1958, Nixon's motorcade was attacked by an angry mob, and he narrowly escaped injury. In a more lighthearted encounter in 1959, Nixon debated Soviet leader Nikita Khrushchev before television cameras. The argument became known as the "Kitchen Debate" because it took place in a model American kitchen at a trade show in Moscow. Nixon became a respected voice in foreign affairs as he turned his keen mind to international problems. To his fiery political style, he added an understanding of the importance of peace between nations.

Nixon served as vice president for eight years. When Eisenhower left the White House in January 1961, the Republicans chose Richard Nixon to be their candidate for president.

Nixon's opponent in 1960 had also been elected to Congress in 1946. He was also a U.S. Navy veteran of World War II. His name was John Fitzgerald Kennedy.

Despite the similarities in their careers, the two candidates were very different. Unlike the near poverty of Nixon's youth, Kennedy's background had been famous and wealthy. Nixon was from California, a western state, while Kennedy was from Massachusetts, in the east. Most important, perhaps, was the difference in their styles. Kennedy was several years younger than Nixon. He appeared more dynamic than his Republican opponent and enjoyed better relations with the press. Kennedy's ready wit and keen smile contrasted with Nixon's sober, serious manner.

The race was one of the closest in U.S. history. Nixon led for most of the campaign. Then, only a few weeks before the election, the two candidates met in a series of televised debates. Nixon, tired from the campaign, looked weary in the debates. The younger, more relaxed Kennedy stole the show. Overnight, Nixon fell behind in the polls.

As the votes were counted on election night, the two candidates were neck and neck. Finally, however, the Democratic ticket gained a slim lead, winning by only a few thousand votes in some states. The next morning, Kennedy was declared the winner.

Nixon now faced an important decision. He and his supporters knew that fraud had taken place at the polls in at least one state. Many advisers urged him to call for an investigation or a recount. Nixon refused to do so. He felt that the strength of the presidency was too important to weaken with an investigation. One of his last duties as vice president was to count the votes of the Electoral College and officially declare John F. Kennedy the next president.

This was the first election Nixon had lost. For the first time in fourteen years, he held no elected office. He spent 1961 writing a book, *Six Crises*, about his political career. He decided to run for governor of California in 1962. He ran against a popular governor, Pat Brown, and lost. The morning after the election, he spoke to reporters. Nixon, bitter in defeat, felt he had lost because of unfair treatment by the press. He announced he was leaving politics: "You won't have Dick Nixon to kick around any more, because, gentlemen, this is my last press conference."

The 1960s were a stormy decade in U.S. history. The cold war with the Soviets and Communist China continued.

A family watches John F. Kennedy making a statement in one of the televised presidential debates of the 1960 campaign.

At least once the world was on the brink of nuclear war. In 1963, President Kennedy was assassinated. The civil rights movement gained national attention as African Americans demanded basic rights that had been too long denied to them.

President Lyndon B. Johnson, who had been Kennedy's vice president, tackled many of the era's issues. He launched government programs to try to solve the nation's social problems and to create what Johnson called the "Great Society." The programs included aid to education, housing for the poor, and the government health program called Medicare. The "Great Society" also meant the growth of the federal government. Some people thought that the Democrats under Johnson had gone too far in their efforts to reshape American society.

But the issue that divided Americans the most was the country's increasing involvement in the Vietnam War. Throughout the decade, the United States committed itself more and more to protecting South Vietnam from its Communist neighbor, North Vietnam. The United States first sent aid, then military advisers, and finally troops. Many Americans felt that the brutal war so far away was no place for Americans to be dying.

President Lyndon Johnson (center) and Vice President Hubert Humphrey (left) discuss the Vietnam War with military advisers in 1968.

Huge protests against U.S. involvement in the fighting marked the election year of 1968. The North Vietnamese and their Vietcong supporters launched the Tet Offensive, a series of surprise attacks on U.S. and South Vietnamese forces. The attacks were beaten back, but the offensive caused many Americans to doubt that the United States could win in Vietnam. The controversy weakened the presidency of Lyndon Johnson, who announced he would not run for reelection.

By now, Richard Nixon felt it was time to return to politics. In the years since his defeats, he had worked in a New York law firm. He had kept in contact with his old political supporters and had made new friends. One was John Mitchell, a law partner who joined Nixon in his political comeback.

The time was never better for a Republican victory than in 1968. The conflicts of the decade had disorganized the Democratic party. Senator Robert Kennedy, a brother of the assassinated president, was a leading contender for the Democratic nomination. Then he was assassinated after an early primary victory in California. George C. Wallace, a Democrat from Alabama, started his own presidential campaign and took many Democratic voters in the South away from the party. In the streets outside the Democratic National Convention in Chicago in the summer of 1968, antiwar protesters battled police while the nation watched on television.

In contrast, the Republican party stood firmly behind its old hero, Richard M. Nixon. In his acceptance speech, Nixon appealed to the "silent majority"—ordinary Americans. Nixon made "law and order" his campaign theme. He hoped to reassure Americans worried about the riots and protests throughout the nation. Nixon's running mate, former Maryland governor Spiro Agnew, took over the job of attacking the Democrats.

Nixon said he had a "secret plan" to end America's involvement in Vietnam, but kept his exact plans to himself. His experienced campaign staff had learned

Richard Nixon is surrounded by antiwar protesters during the 1968 presidential campaign.

Henry Kissinger (fourth from left) speaks to Chinese leader Mao Zedong (third from left) during the talks that led to President Nixon's historic 1972 visit to China.

from the mistakes of 1960. In this election, Nixon decided, there would be no debates.

The Democratic candidate, Hubert H. Humphrey, was a determined campaigner. He made speeches across the country, contrasting his open style with Nixon's careful approach. As it had in 1960, Nixon's lead began to slip.

Nixon and Humphrey were even in the polls for much of the campaign. The voting was close, but on election day Nixon was victorious. He had finally reached his goal—the presidency.

One of the first tasks of a newly elected president is to choose a cabinet. Officials must be appointed to offer advice and carry out the president's orders. In the Nixon White House, the most powerful positions went to the people who had run the presidential campaign. Campaign organizers H. R. (Robert) Haldeman and John Ehrlichman became White House Chief of Staff and Chief Counsel to the President, respectively. Nixon's law partner John Mitchell was appointed attorney general. All three men would play leading roles in the scandal that grew out of the Watergate break-in.

In his first term as president, Nixon often surprised both his friends and his critics. One of these occasions was his trip to China. Although he had based

One of Richard Nixon's happiest tasks as president was welcoming home the Apollo astronauts who became the first men on the moon in July 1969.

his early career on fierce anti-Communist attacks, Nixon felt it was time to open relations with Communist China. In February 1972, he traveled to Beijing, met with China's leaders, and restored contact between the United States and the world's most populous country. Henry Kissinger, one of the brightest stars on Nixon's staff, planned the trip.

Nixon also believed it was important for the United States and the Soviet Union to work together to ease the tensions of the cold war. He traveled to Moscow in 1972 met with the Soviet leader Leonid Brezhnev. The meeting led to a new period of openness between the United States and the Soviet Union, called *détente*.

At home, Nixon faced a Congress in which both houses were controlled by the Democrats. It was the first time in over a hundred years that a president had so little support in the legislature. This division between Congress and the president became important as Watergate became a battle between the executive and legislative branches.

But the main focus of Nixon's first term remained the war in Vietnam. Nixon had promised to achieve "Peace with Honor," but neither victory nor defeat was on the horizon when he took office. The war spread as Nixon used

21

American bombers against enemy bases in Cambodia, a country on the border of South Vietnam. The bombing campaign was kept secret from Congress and the public. When the *New York Times* reported the bombing in May 1970, Nixon was furious that the story had leaked. He ordered illegal wiretaps on newsmen and government employees he suspected in the leaks.

On July 23, a memo written by Federal Bureau of Investigation (FBI) agent Tom C. Huston went out with the president's approval to all American intelligence agencies. It lifted the legal restrictions on spying against American citizens. The Huston memo authorized government agents to open mail, tap telephones, and enter homes without a search warrant. Five days later, John Mitchell and FBI Director J. Edgar Hoover convinced the president to cancel the memo. But to many people who had read the document inside and outside the White House, the president's intent was clear.

That year, U.S. ground forces followed up the air attacks, moving into Cambodia and further widening the war. Later, Nixon's critics would point to the secret bombing and the Huston memo as examples of Nixon's misuse of presidential power.

As the war dragged on, protests at home increased. In 1970, six students were killed in antiwar protests at Kent State and Jackson State universities. A year later, the government was embarrassed when newspapers published a secret government report on the war called the Pentagon Papers. They had been leaked to the press by Daniel Ellsberg, who had worked on the report. Ellsberg instantly became an enemy of the Nixon administration.

The president realized the war had to end. He sent Henry Kissinger to negotiate with the North Vietnamese leaders. At the same time, he began bringing U.S. troops home while continuing to bomb North Vietnam. American forces began turning the burden of the war over to the South Vietnamese army, a process called Vietnamization. The war didn't end, but Nixon's actions won him some public support.

As the next election approached, most politicians felt that Nixon would be reelected. Even though peace in Vietnam had escaped his grasp, Nixon's foreign policy elsewhere had been successful. The Democratic party was again disorganized. The Democratic nominee, George McGovern, had made many mistakes and was slipping in the polls.

When the arrest of the burglars at Democratic National Headquarters was announced, few people knew the effect the news had inside the White House. Within a few hours, a cover-up had already begun.

Wounded men are evacuated from the jungle in Vietnam.

2

THE POWER OF THE PRESIDENT

When the Watergate scandal began, the Nixon White House was almost empty of its most powerful occupants. Chief of Staff Haldeman and the president were in Florida. John Mitchell, Nixon's old friend and manager of his reelection campaign, was in California. Only John Ehrlichman, who had been promoted to chief adviser on domestic affairs, was in Washington. The man who had replaced him as counsel to the president, John W. Dean III, was in the Philippines. (As counsel to the president, Dean acted as Nixon's lawyer.)

As the president's inner circle returned to Washington, they tried to discover who had ordered the Watergate burglary. Some of them knew that Howard Hunt had worked at the White House, but no one was sure when or if he had left.

Nixon had returned from a summit meeting in the Soviet Union only a few weeks before. Compared with the arms control agreement he had reached there, the Watergate burglary was a small matter. He left it to the men around him to deal with the problem.

The president's closest advisers had been hardened by the tough campaigns of Nixon's career. They had learned to play what some called "political hardball." This meant that they were willing to do almost anything to serve their president. Nixon always believed that in politics, tough tactics were necessary. With or without the knowledge of Nixon and his staff, the raid on the Democratic headquarters had sprung from that philosophy.

The president was up for reelection in only a few months. His advisers feared that the scandal might cost him a

E. Howard Hunt, one of the chief figures of the Watergate scandal. Behind him is G. Gordon Liddy.

25

James McCord, one of the five "burglars."

second term as president. They felt it was their job to save Nixon's campaign. Without any long-range plan on how to weather the crisis, the cover-up began.

From the very first days of the scandal, the efforts of reporters, government investigators, and politicians who tried to discover the truth were frustrated. The power of the presidency was used to slow or halt all investigations into Watergate. At times, it seemed to those both inside and outside the White House that the full story would never be told.

The five burglars were loyal to the men who had hired them. When they were arrested, they gave false names to the police. They also refused to talk about why they had committed the crime or who had ordered it. Their identities had to be learned from the letters, address books, and other papers they carried.

The day after the break-in, investigators discovered that James McCord worked as a security consultant for Nixon's campaign committee. The Committee to Re-elect the President (called CRP, or "Creep," throughout Washington) worked separately from the Republican National Committee. The organization was tightly controlled by the White House. CRP admitted that McCord worked for them but denied any knowledge of the break-in. The committee claimed that McCord had many other employers. Their statements suggested that another of McCord's clients must have ordered the break-in.

Something else, however, pointed to the White House. This was Howard Hunt's name and phone number, found in one of the burglars' address books. Howard Hunt was a political consultant who had once worked at the White House. The *Washington Post* reported Hunt's association with the burglars on June 19, 1972. The story's writer, reporter Bob Woodward, telephoned Hunt before he had learned any details about the arrests. Hunt's only comment before hanging up was "Good God!" A few days later he fled the country.

After the first news stories, the Democratic party quickly seized the opportunity to criticize its Republican opponents. Party chairman Lawrence F. O'Brien, whose office had been burglarized, challenged the Republicans' denials. He said, "No mere statement of innocence by Nixon's campaign manager, John Mitchell, will dispel these questions." O'Brien filed a lawsuit against CRP for $1 million and called for a full investigation of the matter by the Justice Department.

On June 1, the chairman of CRP, John Mitchell, quietly resigned. He said he was leaving the position for personal reasons.

The case against the burglars was given to a prosecutor, Earl Silbert, and a federal grand jury. (A grand jury has the power to indict—charge—people for a crime if it feels there is enough evidence.) The FBI began its own investigation. The acting director of the FBI, L. Patrick Gray, said that 150 agents were trying to find Howard Hunt.

As in many criminal investigations, the results of this operation were kept secret at first. It was the press that made the next discovery. The *New York Times* reported on July 25, 1972, that it had the phone records of one of the burglars, Bernard L. Barker. Barker had called a lawyer at the Committee to Re-elect the President, G. Gordon Liddy, fifteen times in the months before the break-in. The *Times* story also said that $114,000 had been given to Barker two months before the break-in. The money came

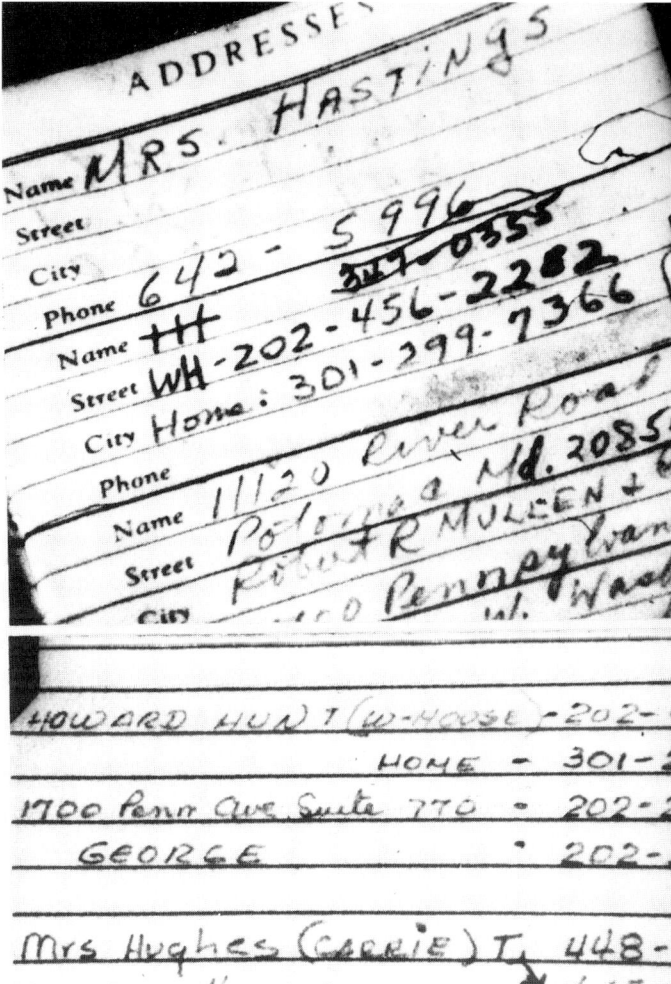

Hunt's White House phone number was found in an address book on one of the burglars caught breaking into the Democratic National Committee's headquarters in the Watergate complex.

from a bank in Mexico, but no one was sure who had originally deposited it. Suspicion soon came to rest on Liddy and CRP.

Two young reporters who had worked on the story from the beginning soon thought they had the answer. They were Bob Woodward, who had

G. Gordon Liddy, lawyer for CRP.

first found Howard Hunt, and Carl Bernstein, both of the *Washington Post*. They discovered that one of the checks from Mexico had been signed by Kenneth H. Dahlberg. Dahlberg had been Nixon's campaign manager in the 1968 election. When Woodward and Bernstein called Dahlberg, he admitted signing over the $25,000 check, made up of campaign contributions, to the Committee to Re-elect the President. For the first time, it looked as though someone in CRP had paid the burglars. The story broke on August 1, almost six weeks after the arrests.

The news led to still more investigations. Congress had passed a law only a few months before that stated how campaign contributions and expenses were to be reported. The $25,000 from Dahlberg hadn't been reported, which was against the new law. The federal government's General Accounting Office (the agency that oversees government spending) began an audit—a financial investigation—of CRP. Then Congress's Committee on Banking and Currency decided to look into the financial part of the scandal. Soon it was clear that the Dahlberg contribution was not the only questionable gift to the Nixon campaign. Later, in 1973, the Justice Department was to discover that CRP had not reported a $200,000 campaign contribution from financier Robert Vesco. At the time, Vesco was under investigation for stealing over $200 million from U.S. banks.

The difference between these investigations and the others begun by the government is important. The Justice Department and the FBI are part of the executive branch, and their directors report to the president. For the first four years of his term, Nixon had appointed loyal Republicans to those positions. Many Democrats thought that if the White House was behind the break-in, the investigations run by the executive branch might be unsuccessful on purpose. At the least, they could be delayed so that no embarrassing results emerged until after the election. The Democrats, however, controlled Congress. The audit and the House committee investigation began in earnest. Already, a contest between the powers of the presidency and those of Congress was beginning.

In only a few weeks, the General Accounting Office released its report on the finances of the Committee to Re-elect the President. It found that at least $350,000 had gone into a secret "slush fund" used for unreported activities. Officials of CRP claimed that they didn't know how the money had been spent. The White House said that the matter would be investigated.

From the first reports of the burglary, the White House had declined to answer questions, saying that the break-in was not worth commenting on. As the scandal grew, the White House had stuck to this strategy of "stonewalling"—neither denying nor confirming any of the stories. The president's advisers decided that the best response would be to ignore the matter for as long as possible.

Behind the scenes, however, the White House was doing everything it could to keep the scandal from growing. John Dean took charge of the contents of Howard Hunt's safe. The safe contained evidence of many of the dirty tricks planned by Nixon's aides. H. R. Haldeman destroyed many documents that connected the White House with the men who had planned the break-in. Nixon told Haldeman to ask the Central Intelligence Agency for help in stalling the FBI investigation.

At the Justice Department, the investigation was kept under tight control. The attorney general, Richard G. Kleindienst, had been appointed by President Nixon only a few months before. Until that time, Kleindienst had served under Attorney General John Mitchell, an old friend of the president's. Mitchell was now the head of the Committee to Re-elect the President. Kleindienst told Prosecutor Earl Silbert to concentrate on the crime itself. Silbert narrowed his investigation to the five burglars, G. Gordon Liddy, and Howard Hunt, who had returned to the United States to give himself up.

When Silbert and the grand jury interviewed employees of CRP, their questions kept the focus away from finding out who at the committee had hired the burglars. Some of these employees felt that the law had been abused. Frustrated by the jury's limited questions, they went back to give more information. They were all but ignored.

The scope of the investigation also angered Judge John J. Sirica, chief judge of the U.S. District Court for Washington, D.C., who was presiding over the case. He asked the burglars again and again why they had tried to bug the Democrats. The defendants remained silent.

At the FBI, the influence of the presidency was also strongly felt. Like Attorney General Kleindienst, L. Patrick Gray had recently been appointed by the president. Gray was instructed to turn over FBI progress reports of the investigation to the Counsel for the President, John W. Dean. Since the president was the chief law enforcement official in

29

Judge John J. Sirica.

the country, Gray couldn't refuse. Dean used the reports to keep track of the investigation. He knew whom the FBI agents planned to interview and what questions they would ask. Often, he would conduct an interview with CRP employees before the FBI. This prepared them for the questions that were coming.

On August 22, the Republican party nominated Richard Nixon to run again for president. The convention was a jubilant event. Nixon enjoyed the full support of his party. His lead over Democratic candidate George McGovern grew bigger every day. The Watergate stories that appeared in the nation's newspapers were confusing to many people, and so far little had been proved. It was still not known who had ordered the break-in. Few people thought the president had known about the criminals in his campaign committee's pay. Outside of Washington, the scandal was hardly news.

The same day that Nixon received his party's nomination, the judge hearing the Democratic chairman's $1 million suit made a surprising announcement. He said that publicity caused by the lawsuit might make it impossible for the burglars to get a fair trial. Therefore, the court records of the lawsuit would be kept secret. The evidence would be sealed until after the burglars' trial—and after the election. The judge who made the ruling, Charles Richney, hadn't been asked to do this by either side in the case. He, too, had been appointed by President Nixon.

A week after his nomination, Nixon made his first public statement about the Watergate matter. He admitted that there had been "technical violations" of campaign law. He insisted, however, that the violations had occurred on both sides. About the burglary, he added, "What really hurts in matters of this sort is not the fact that they occur, because overzealous people in campaigns do things wrong. What really hurts is if you try to cover it up."

On September 15, two months after the break-in, the burglars, Hunt, and Liddy were indicted for burglary, theft, and planting surveillance devices. The burglars' names were Bernard Barker, Virgilio R. Gonzalez, Eugenio R. Martinez, James W. McCord, Jr., and Frank A. Sturgis. All except McCord were from Miami, where they were involved with groups of exiled Cubans who hoped to overthrow Cuban dictator Fidel Castro. Many people assumed that the burglars had CIA connections, but there was little hard evidence of that. The case against the seven men was narrowly defined. There was no mention of secret campaign funds, of a political conspiracy, or of who had ordered the break-in. On those questions, the burglars remained silent.

Starting only a few days after the arrests, however, the defendants had demanded a price for their silence. None of them was wealthy, and their legal costs were high. Hunt and the burglars turned to Liddy for money, and Liddy turned to the White House. The network that had originally provided the secret funds for the break-in was again in action. Money was quietly raised and handed over to Hunt by the president's personal lawyer, Herbert W. Kalmbach. By the time the first week of the trial was over, $220,000 had been paid. The secret dealings took their toll on Kalmbach, who had known nothing of the burglary before handling the money. Soon he resigned rather than continue the payoffs.

Besides the burglars' growing demands for money, everything seemed under control. The congressional committee investigating CRP's finances voted against giving its chairman the power to subpoena. This meant that no one from the White House could be ordered to answer questions before the committee. The Republicans on the committee had all voted against the chairman, and John Dean had instructed the Justice Department to protest the hearings. The Republicans were joined by a few Democrats who had felt the influence of the White House. Without the power to subpoena, the chairman held hearings in which Nixon's advisers were represented by empty chairs.

It was not until mid-October, with the election a few weeks away, that the next bombshells burst. *Time* magazine and the *Washington Post* reported that Kalmbach had paid lawyer Donald H. Segretti $35,000 to run a campaign of "dirty tricks" against the Democrats. Many of the tricks had merely been pranks—like having unwanted pizzas delivered to Democratic rallies and fund-raising events. Some of the tricks, however, were more harmful. They focused especially on the Democratic campaigns in the primaries. The operatives in charge of this secret campaign would often send out insulting or racist press releases on the stationery of Democratic candidates. The purpose was to divide the Democratic party before the election.

The stories said that these "dirty tricks" had been a basic strategy of the

A "bug" being placed into a telephone. Planting surveillance devices like this was one of CRP's "dirty tricks."

Nixon reelection campaign. The stories agreed that this kind of political "hardball" had been a part of politics for a long time but that the scale and organization of the Nixon effort was unlike any before.

The Nixon White House finally went on the offensive. Within hours, they called the stories "fiction and absurdities." The *Washington Post*, which had tracked the Watergate story closely from the beginning, was singled out as a target for the counterattack. In television appearances, before live audiences, and in press releases, Republicans such as Senator Robert Dole attacked the newspaper. They accused the paper of siding with George McGovern and trying to damage President Nixon's reputation.

Nixon's supporters had heard him attack the press before. Since the days of his fight to prosecute Alger Hiss, Nixon believed that the newspapers of the nation disliked him. He still remembered how eagerly the newspapers had headlined the "slush fund" stories of 1952, when he was a vice-presidential candidate. He often said that his loss to

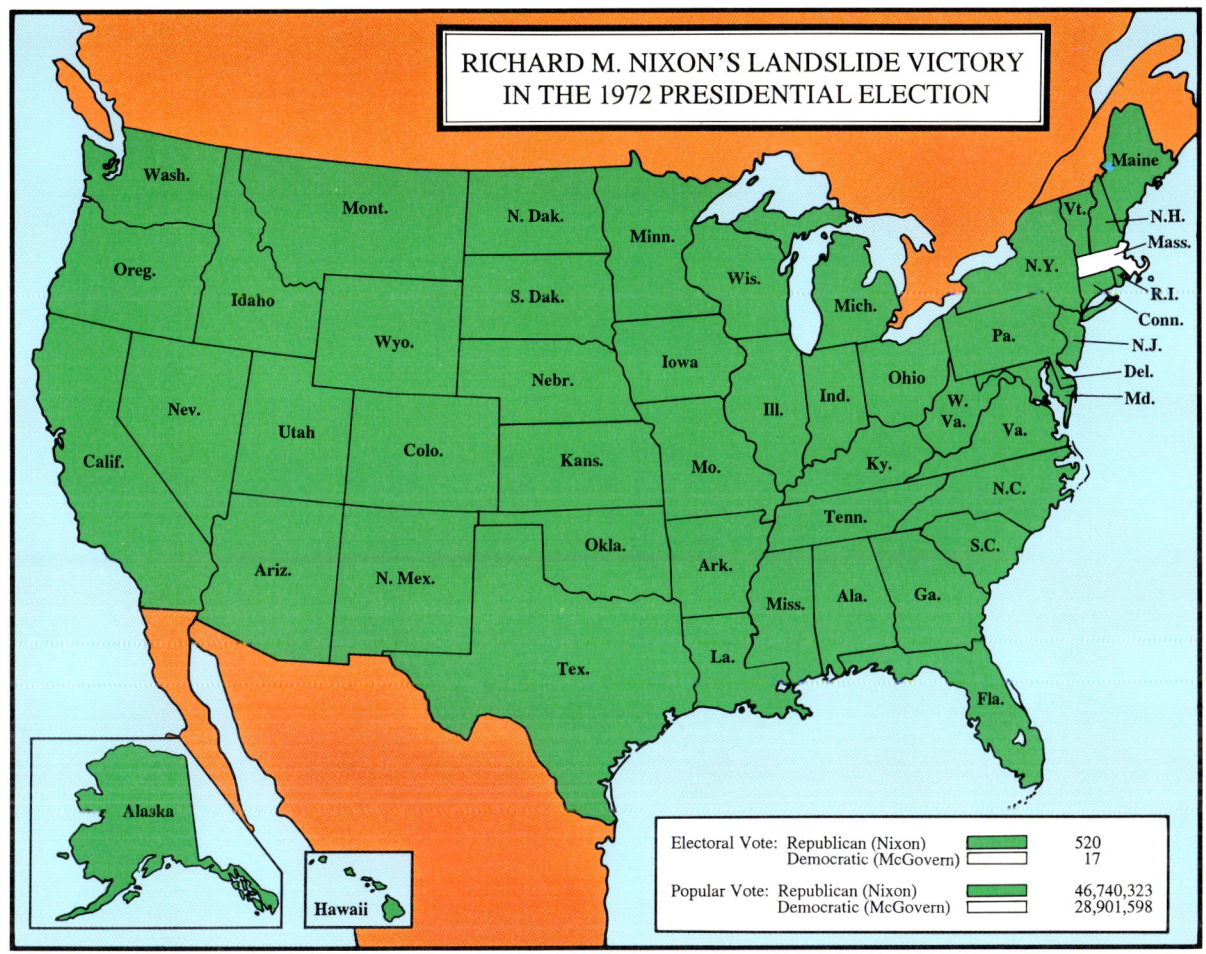

Kennedy in 1960 wouldn't have happened if the press had been fair to him. Many voters also thought that anti-Nixon newspapers exaggerated the Watergate scandal.

By November 7, election day, there was little doubt that the president would be reelected. Most voters judged his first term a success, and the Democrats' campaign had been disorganized. When the ballots were counted, Nixon had won in a landslide. It was the greatest victory of any Republican presidential candidate in history up to that time.

Finally, the Nixon White House hoped it could forget about Watergate. With the power of the presidency his for four more years, Nixon seemed sure to escape the scandal altogether. Only a few more problems remained. A committee under Senator Edward Kennedy had begun its own investigation. Also, the burglars were still on trial and still demanding money for their silence. But the public had shown their trust in the president with a landslide victory. There was little reason to believe that this trust could be shaken.

3

"WHAT DID THE PRESIDENT KNOW?"

The months before Nixon's second inauguration passed with little mention of Watergate. The war in Vietnam remained the big issue. In an effort to force North Vietnam to agree to a settlement, Nixon decided to begin relentlessly bombing Hanoi, North Vietnam's capital. He also approved the mining of Haiphong, an important North Vietnamese harbor.

Meanwhile, the grand jury went back to work in secret. The newspapers found little new to report about Watergate after the election. Senator Edward Kennedy's investigation had been stalled, but the Senate had appointed a new committee to look into the affair. Its leader would be an old and respected senator, Samuel Ervin of North Carolina. The Senate Select Watergate Committee would not begin hearings until May 1973.

Months before the committee began its work, however, the scandal returned to haunt the White House. In January 1973, Nixon appointed acting FBI directory L. Patrick Gray to become the permanent head of the bureau. The Senate, which had to confirm the nomination, quickly made the FBI's handling of Watergate an issue. Gray surprised the Senate by reporting that he had turned the files of the investigation over to John Dean. The senators decided to call Dean to testify. President Nixon protested. He said that close aides of the president weren't required to answer to the Senate. This angered the Democrats in Congress, but the issue remained unresolved.

Only two months into the president's second term, the wall of conspiracy that had surrounded the scandal began to tumble down. On March 23, 1973, the

Chief Justice Warren Burger swears in Richard Nixon for a second term as president on January 20, 1973.

The members of the Senate Select Committee on Watergate. The chairman, Sam Ervin of North Carolina, is seated at center.

silence of the burglars was broken. On that day, a large crowd gathered in Judge Sirica's courtroom. The people present had come to hear the sentencing of Hunt, Liddy, and the Watergate burglars. Liddy and James McCord had been found guilty by a jury on January 23, and the other five had pleaded guilty. The men had maintained their silence for nine months, but Judge Sirica had offered them another chance to speak out before passing sentence.

When he entered the courtroom, Sirica announced that he had received a letter from James McCord. Judge Sirica read the letter before an open court packed with reporters. In it, McCord said that he wanted to discuss the details of Watergate. He made it clear that he wouldn't speak to an FBI agent or a Justice Department official—only to Sirica himself. Although McCord's letter revealed no details, it made serious charges. McCord claimed that "political pressure" had caused the defendants to plead guilty and remain silent. He also said that witnesses at the trial had committed perjury by lying to protect the people who had ordered the break-in. McCord said that he, his family, and

36

Senator Howard Baker of Tennessee, the committee's highest-ranking Republican member, with Senator Sam Ervin of North Carolina.

friends might be in danger if he spoke out.

When Sirica finished, the crowd, which had listened in shocked silence, gasped. Reporters rushed to telephones to call their newspapers. Watergate was a national story again.

Now that McCord was willing to testify, the Senate Watergate Committee offered him a chance to speak publicly. In McCord's testimony, they saw their first chance to unravel the mystery around Watergate. The members of the committee had been carefully chosen to show that both parties wanted to get to the bottom of the scandal. There were four Democrats and three Republicans on the committee. Sam Ervin of North Carolina, the Democratic chairman, and Howard H. Baker of Tennessee, the senior Republican, were both greatly respected on Capitol Hill. The other members were all in their first terms as senators. This made it seem unlikely that any committee member might use the publicity from the investigation to launch a presidential campaign. The Senate didn't want it to look as though it was attacking the White House for political gain. The Republicans on the committee wanted to show that they were not covering up the truth to save Nixon's presidency. The Democrats wanted to prove that the charges against the president had been made for the good of the country, not just for party politics.

The committee was not a jury. It couldn't convict anyone of a crime. Its only duty was to find out the full truth behind Watergate. For this purpose, the committee had two powerful weapons. One was the power of subpoena, which allowed the committee to order any person with evidence to appear and answer questions. The only limit on this power was that witnesses didn't have to give information that would incriminate themselves—a right guaranteed by the Fifth Amendment to the Constitution. The other weapon was the power to grant *immunity from prosecution*. Witnesses with immunity could freely testify about crimes they had committed, because their testimony could not be used against them in any later trial.

McCord's first meeting with representatives of the committee came only a few days after his letter was read aloud in court. In the secret meeting, he named two conspirators who he said were involved in the burglary and cover-up. John Dean was one. Jeb Magruder, second-in-charge of CRP, was the second. Until now, there had been no evidence that anyone was involved except Liddy, Hunt, McCord, Sturgis, and the Cubans. Now, a top White House aide and an important official at CRP had been linked to the break-in.

The committee quickly subpoenaed Dean and Magruder. At first, the White House insisted that Dean, a White House aide, couldn't be subpoenaed by the Senate. The president said that members of the executive branch had "executive privilege," which protected them from the power of the Senate. This theory was based on the Constitution's separation of powers, under which all three branches of government are considered equal. Since the executive branch was equal with the legislative, the president's lawyers argued, the Congress could not subpoena the White House staff the way it might ordinary citizens.

The power of executive privilege is meant to protect those whose job it is to offer the president frank advice. This privilege had been claimed by presidents from George Washington to Harry Truman. Since the members of the committee didn't want to appear hostile to the president, they negotiated quietly with the White House. On April 17, Nixon reversed his position and ordered his aides to cooperate with the committee. The president didn't want to look as if he was hiding the truth.

On April 26, the *New York Post* ran a story that further battered the White House. According to the story, L. Patrick Gray, acting FBI director at the time, had destroyed evidence found in Howard Hunt's White House safe. The day after the story appeared, Gray resigned.

That same day, Hunt and Liddy were charged in another burglary. In September 1971, they had broken into the of-

Robert Haldeman testifying before the Senate Select Committee on Watergate.

fices of a psychiatrist treating Daniel Ellsberg, the man who had leaked the Pentagon Papers to the press. It was well known that Nixon's two most important aides, Haldeman and Ehrlichman, hated Ellsberg. The burglary suggested that Watergate was only one of many operations authorized by someone in the Nixon administration.

On April 30, only two weeks before the Senate committee planned to begin public hearings, the impact of the growing scandal on the White House began to show. On that day, Haldeman, Ehrlichman, and Attorney General Kliendienst all resigned. They said that the reports of their involvement in Watergate had made it impossible for them to go on serving the president. On the same day, Nixon fired John Dean, who was cooperating with the grand jury and Senator Ervin's committee.

That night, President Nixon went on television and admitted that mistakes had been made at the White House. He claimed that he had been kept in the dark along with the rest of the nation. But Nixon said he took full responsibility for what had happened. The president ended by saying, "I must now turn my full attention to the larger duties of this office." Nixon still thought that Watergate might end quietly. He hoped that this speech would end the crisis as the "Checkers Speech" had in 1952.

Watergate and the related scandals would not go away, however. Daniel Ellsberg's trial came to a dramatic end on May 11. The case was dismissed because the government had illegally tapped Ellsberg's phone for more than a year. It was also known that John Ehrlichman had twice met with federal judge Mathew Byrne, who was presiding over the trial. Government interference in the trial was the official reason given for the dismissal.

When the Ervin committee opened its hearings on May 17, the events of the previous weeks had raised public interest in the scandal to new heights. The hearings, conducted by the senators and their chief counsel, Samuel Dash, were televised from beginning to end.

After a session describing the arrest of the burglars, James McCord took the witness stand. McCord added a new twist to his charges against Dean and Magruder. He said that before his trial, Liddy had promised him an executive pardon if he pleaded guilty. This seemed to mean the White House was involved in the cover-up, because only the president could offer such a pardon.

The next witness to testify was Jeb Magruder of CRP. He confirmed what McCord had said, admitted his own perjury before the Watergate grand jury, and added another name to the list of those involved—John Mitchell. Mitchell had been the head of CRP, and before that, the attorney general of the United States. The nation's top law enforcement official had been linked to a crime. Now, people asked openly if the president might be involved. The man who might know for sure was the next witness to appear before the committee—the president's counsel, John Dean.

Dean was scheduled to appear on June 18. Suddenly, objections were raised. A few weeks before, the president had appointed a special prosecutor to look into Watergate. This prosecutor, Archibald Cox, was supposed to work independently of the executive branch. Finally, people thought, the grand jury would be guided by someone without ties to the president.

Cox, however, began fighting to keep Dean's testimony from being heard. The special prosecutor felt that the coverage given his appearance would make it hard for Dean and others to receive a fair trial. If a judge later decided that a fair trial was impossible, there might be no trial at all. Cox thought that a criminal trial was more important than the Senate's "political" trial. The Senate's Watergate Committee, however, argued that it was more important to get at the truth behind the scandal than to convict criminals. The nation's confidence in its government was at stake.

Judge Sirica sided with the Watergate Committee against Cox. Dean would testify.

Even so, Dean's appearance didn't begin as scheduled. A few months before, when still on the White House staff, Dean had met with the president before a meeting with Howard Baker. In

President Nixon speaks to the nation on television on April 30, 1973.

the meeting, Nixon had asked Baker about the committee's investigation. Dean suspected that Baker would prepare the White House for what Dean might reveal. Dean decided not to discuss his testimony with the committee until just before his appearance. This way the White House wouldn't have time to plan a counterattack against Dean's testimony.

Dean met with the Republican committee members privately only two days before his appearance. He freely told them what he knew about Nixon's involvement in Watergate. Then, on the morning of his scheduled appearance, Howard Baker made a motion before the committee. Because the president was on an important diplomatic trip to the Soviet Union, Baker suggested delaying the hearings for a week. The senators didn't want to embarrass the president during his meeting the Soviet leaders. The motion passed.

The week's delay wasn't a pleasant one for Dean. Details of his testimony to the Republicans had leaked to the press, but only parts damaging to Dean. The leaks revealed that it was Dean who had ordered Hunt to flee the country after the scandal broke. Dean had also borrowed $4,000 from the "slush fund" to help pay for a honeymoon with his wife, Maureen.

The White House press office quickly released its own version of the events

41

John Dean is sworn in before the Senate Select Committee.

about which Dean would testify. Newspapers accused Dean of lying before he had even spoken. The public grew angry at Dean, who seemed to be attacking the president. In the middle of the week, the committee received a threat against Dean's life.

By the time he finally reached the stand, interest in Dean's testimony was high. Dean took the entire first day of his testimony to read his 245-page opening statement. The story it told shocked the nation.

For the first time, the world of Richard Nixon's White House was laid bare. According to Dean, the Watergate burglary had been only one operation in a greater pattern of criminal abuse of power.

For four years, said Dean, the White House had used the powers of the presidency to attack political enemies. Citizens who disagreed with the Nixon administration's policies had been spied on and harassed. Reporters who wrote stories critical of the White House were singled out for tax investigations. A special group called the "plumbers" had been formed to find out which members of the White House staff were giving these reporters their information. And the White House kept an "enemies list" of people on whom the president's men wanted revenge. The election-year campaign against the Democrats was just the political side of a campaign that included many agencies in the executive branch. In the Watergate cover-up, the White House had simply used its authority to defend itself.

Dean supported his charges with official documents that he had saved at his house. After he was fired, he had put these papers in a safety deposit box and given the key to Judge Sirica. The documents, and Dean's impressive memory for details, made his story more believable.

Dean claimed to have discussed the cover-up with President Nixon in several meetings. The first of these was on September 15, 1972, two months after the arrests at the Watergate. Dean had told the president how he and others at the White House had handled the cover-up so far. Another important meeting took place on March 21, 1973. At this meeting, Nixon agreed that $1 million should be raised to buy the burglars' continued silence. Dean had dealt with the president mostly through Haldeman and Ehrlichman. He based the charges against Nixon himself on these two encounters.

After his opening statement, Dean faced the committee for four days of questioning. The Republicans focused on the meetings, which were the only evidence against the president himself. Senator Baker asked a question that would be repeated throughout the nation: What did the president know and when did he know it?

The Nixon administration attacked Dean's version of the two meetings. According to the White House, the March 21, 1973, meeting had been the first the president had known about the cover-up. In the White House version, the president had rejected the burglars' blackmail.

Dean's testimony was the greatest blow the Nixon White House had yet suffered. Finally, the president himself had been directly accused. Polls showed that 70 percent of TV viewers believed Dean's version of events. But the basic question remained: What had the president known? It was the word of John Dean against the word of Richard Nixon.

Then, only a few weeks after Dean's appearance, the committee made a surprising discovery. Members of the committee's staff conducted a routine interview of Alexander Butterfield, a former aide to Robert Haldeman. They asked Butterfield how the White House had come up with its version of the meetings between Dean and the president. He replied that the meetings had probably been recorded on tape.

Butterfield explained that the White House had been equipped with a recording system. The system had recorded every conversation in the presidential offices since early in 1971. Butterfield himself had helped install the system.

Finally, the committee had found something it could use to determine the president's guilt or innocence. Somewhere in the White House were tapes of the meetings between Dean and Nixon. The tapes would show which of the men was lying, and whether the president of the United States had been involved in a criminal conspiracy.

The Senate committee quickly decided to ask Nixon to hand over the White House tapes. But what if the president refused?

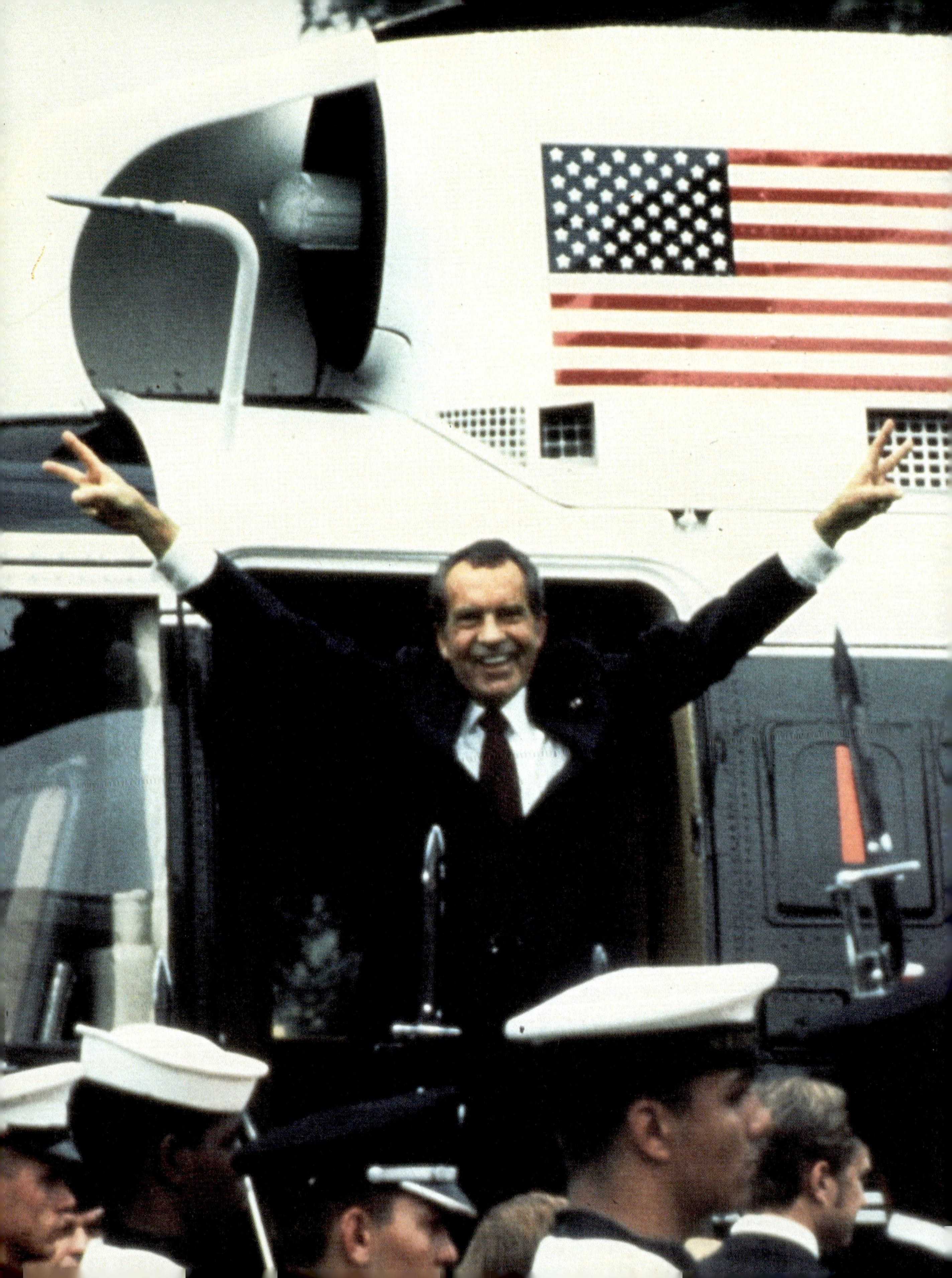

4

THE FALL OF A PRESIDENT

The struggle between the White House and Congress narrowed to a single issue: the White House tapes. To the Senate Select Committee on Watergate, these tapes represented the best way to get at the truth behind Watergate. But the White House considered the tapes to be the property of the executive branch. They revealed the inner workings of the Nixon administration. For the sake of national security, the president and his advisers believed, the tapes should not be given up.

The Senate committee took its request directly to the president. On July 17, 1973, Congress requested tapes of the important conversations directly from the White House. President Nixon refused. That afternoon, the committee voted to subpoena the tapes.

Richard Nixon boards the helicopter that will carry him from the White House after his resignation.

Special Prosecutor Archibald Cox also subpoenaed tapes on July 17. Cox said they were important for the grand jury's criminal investigation. No one had ever subpoenaed the president of the United States before, and now Nixon had been served two subpoenas in one day. The White House refused to obey either, saying that neither Congress nor the special prosecutor had the right to demand evidence from the executive branch.

The Senate Committee now faced a difficult question. They could find the president in contempt of Congress—a serious legal charge. But who would arrest him? The president controlled the Department of Justice, the FBI, and the armed forces. The committee had to find another way to get the tapes. The grand jury and Cox had decided to sue for the tapes in federal court. The committee followed the special prosecutor's lead.

45

E. Howard Hunt speaks before the committee.

The two lawsuits both went to the court of Judge John Sirica, who had presided over the trials of the Watergate burglars. The judge decided in favor of Cox, charging the president to turn over the tapes to the special prosecutor's office. The White House appealed the decision, and the case went to the Federal Court of Appeals. Sirica rejected the Watergate Committee's request, however. The senators had made Watergate a national story. Now the power of the president to refuse to give evidence had stopped them.

In July, the president's former aides appeared before the committee. Without the evidence of the tapes to contradict them, the witnesses were able to "stonewall" the investigation, as the president's men had all along. Former Attorney General John Mitchell claimed to remember little of the events surrounding the Watergate break-in. John Ehrlichman attacked the committee in long speeches that seldom answered the committee's questions. Robert Haldeman also claimed not to remember much. But he said he had listened to one of the subpoenaed tapes—the March 21, 1973, meeting between Dean and the president. He said that the tape proved the president's innocence. The former White House chief of staff was calling Dean a liar.

Attention soon shifted from the work of the committee. Vice President Spiro Agnew, under investigation for taking bribes, resigned from office—another scandal to shake the public's confidence. Nixon nominated House Republican leader Gerald Ford as the new vice president.

On October 15, the court of appeals upheld Judge Sirica's ruling and demanded that the president turn over the subpoenaed tapes to Special Prosecutor Archibald Cox. The White House decided to offer Cox a compromise. Rather than the actual tapes, they offered transcripts—written versions of the taped conversations. These transcripts would be edited by the president so that no national security secrets would be revealed. A respected senator, John C.

A New Vice President

Spiro Agnew immediately following his resignation.

Just as Watergate began to dominate President Nixon's second term, another scandal in the White House shocked the nation. In August, the Justice Department revealed that it had been investigating Vice President Spiro T. Agnew. The investigators suspected Agnew of taking large bribes in return for government contracts. The charges covered Agnew's early political career as a county official, as governor of Maryland, and as vice president.

When Nixon selected Agnew as his running mate in 1968, Agnew was not a national figure. He soon became Nixon's spokesman on the subjects of Vietnam, law and order, and the press. He viciously attacked those who disagreed with the president. In many ways, he was a political warrior for Nixon much as Nixon had been for Eisenhower. His special target was the press, which he accused of having an anti-Nixon, "radical liberal" bias.

The Agnew scandal did not last long. About to be indicted for taking bribes, Agnew resigned on October 10, 1973. He agreed to plead "no contest" to tax evasion. Though never imprisoned, he was forced to pay large fines. Nixon chose Gerald R. Ford, the Republican leader in the House of Representatives, as the new vice president. Under the Twenty-fifth Amendment to the Constitution, both houses of Congress confirmed Ford's appointment.

Although Agnew's crimes weren't part of Watergate, they added to suspicions about the Nixon White House. A crisis in confidence, in which the country would lose trust in its leaders, was beginning. The resignation of the vice president helped set the stage for the eventual fall of President Nixon himself.

Leon Jaworski, the special prosecutor who succeeded Archibald Cox.

Stennis of Mississippi, would then compare the tapes with the written transcripts in private. This compromise would maintain the privacy of conversations in the White House.

Cox refused the deal. He wanted the unedited tapes. On Saturday, October 20, Cox held a press conference. Although the president had ordered him not to subpoena any more tapes, Cox said he would do so. If the president refused, Cox would press to find him in contempt of court.

President Nixon was furious. Cox, an employee of the executive branch, was challenging the authority of the president. Nixon ordered Attorney General Elliot Richardson to fire Cox. Richardson refused, saying that the special prosecutor had been appointed to investigate Watergate independently of White House control. Richardson met with the president and offered his resignation. It was accepted.

Richardson's deputy attorney general, William D. Ruckelshaus, was now ordered to fire Cox. He also refused and was fired. The third-ranking Justice Department official, Solicitor General Robert H. Bork, was now the acting attorney general. Bork, at last, agreed to fire Cox. In one day, Nixon had forced out his two top law-enforcement officials and the special prosecutor. FBI agents were sent to seal the offices and files of the three ousted men. The newspapers dubbed the event of October 20, 1973, the "Saturday Night Massacre."

Many Americans were furious. The White House received 250,000 telegrams in a matter of a few days. Almost all were angry at the president's attack on the Justice Department. The Senate Watergate Committee received even more telegrams. Many people now said that the president should be impeached.

Impeachment is the legal process by which Congress can bring the president to trial. According to Article II, Section 4, of the Constitution, if found guilty of treason, bribery, or "high crimes and misdemeanors," the president can be removed from office. The impeachment

An October 1973 anti-Nixon protest in front of the White House.

process is spelled out in Article 1, Section 3, of the Constitution: the House of Representatives votes to impeach the president. An impeached president is tried by the Senate, with the chief justice of the United States presiding over the trial. Only one president had ever been impeached before. This was Andrew Johnson, who had been impeached in 1868 after firing a cabinet member. But the Senate had acquitted Johnson—found him not guilty—by one vote.

After the wave of protest, Nixon retreated from his stubborn stand. He agreed to deliver the tapes to Sirica's court and to appoint a new special prosecutor. Leon Jaworski, a well-known lawyer, was offered the position. He accepted on one condition—that the president could not fire him as he had fired Cox. The White House, caught in the storm of the nation's anger, agreed.

As the president's lawyers prepared the tapes for delivery to the special prosecutor, they made a startling discovery. One of the subpoenaed tapes, containing a conversation between Haldeman and Nixon, was partly erased. The 18-minute gap soon came to

49

Rose Mary Woods, Nixon's secretary. She claimed that she accidentally erased the missing portions of the most famous Watergate tape.

symbolize all that remained hidden about the Watergate affair. Rose Mary Woods, the president's secretary, claimed that she had accidentally erased the tape while transcribing it. A panel of electronics experts analyzed the tape. They decided that it had been erased on purpose.

As the country lost more and more faith in the president, Congress began to question Nixon's conduct of the Vietnam War. A cease-fire agreement signed in January 1973 finally ended the long U.S. involvement in the conflict. Some congressional leaders proposed placing a limit on the presidential power to start military actions. In November, Congress voted to pass the War Powers Act over Nixon's veto. The act limited the president's power to send U.S. forces into combat without congressional approval. Just as the Watergate crisis raised constitutional questions about the balance of power between the branches of the government, the constitutionality of the War Powers Act is still debated today.

Another source of conflict between the executive and legislative branches centered on impoundment. Impoundment occurs when a president uses his veto power to block spending bills that would provide money for programs the president doesn't support. Because the votes of two-thirds of the members of each house of Congress are needed to overturn a presidential veto, impoundment provides the president with a way of determining how federal money is used, even though the Constitution doesn't give the president the power to authorize spending. Nixon had used this process several times—too many times, some in the Democrat-controlled Congress believed. In 1974, Congress passed the Budget and Impoundment Control Act, which limited the executive branch's power to impound funds. As with the War Powers Act, critics charged that the Budget and Impoundment Act went against the Constitution's separation of powers.

In January 1974, the Judiciary Committee of the House of Representatives, under Chairman Peter Rodino, began its own investigation. This new committee was still not able to get at the tapes, which were part of Jaworski's secret grand jury investigation. The committee began to assemble all the evience revealed by the many other investigations.

In the last week of February, the grand jury indicted seven more Watergate conspirators, including Robert Haldeman, John Ehrlichman, and John Mitchell. The men were indicted for conspiracy, obstruction of justice, and perjury. In a secret report to Judge Sirica, the jury named Richard Nixon as an unindicted co-conspirator in the Watergate cover-up. The jury had wanted to indict Richard Nixon, but Jaworski was reluctant to attack the president directly. He felt that under the Constitution, only the Congress had the right to charge the president with a crime. He decided instead to give the report, and the tapes so far received, to the House Judiciary Committee. Finally, Congress was to get the evidence it needed to begin impeachment.

On April 11, the White House was again threatened by subpoenas. Special Prosecutor Jaworski demanded sixty-nine more tapes, and the House Judiciary Committee voted to subpoena forty-two. The tapes covered the whole range of the scandal. If they were released, nothing would remain of the president's claim of executive privilege.

The White House decided on a new strategy. So far, Nixon had reacted to the court challenges one at a time. Each new discovery built suspicion that more was hidden. Now, Nixon felt that a single dramatic act might finally end the scandal. He would release all the subpoenaed tapes to the public. Then he could claim that the whole truth had been revealed.

The White House worked furiously on the project. The tapes were transcribed. President Nixon personally edited the transcripts. The administration claimed that the transcripts contained everything on the tapes except material that might threaten national security. The president and his advisers hoped that the special prosecutor, Congress,

51

and the public would be impressed by the president's honesty.

On April 29, 1974, when the work was done, Nixon made another television appearance. He sat next to a table piled high with the elegantly bound transcripts. He stated that he wanted to clear up the controversy once and for all. He warned that some of the tapes were embarrassing, but said, "Everything is included, the rough as well as the smooth. . . . I am placing my trust in the basic fairness of the American people."

The reaction to the speech was positive, especially among the Republican senators and representatives that Nixon would need on his side to fight impeachment. Republican leaders were glad that the president had given up his stand on executive privilege in order to get the country past Watergate. He had finally admitted his past mistakes and was ready to work with the investigations rather than against them.

The next day, the transcripts of the tapes were released. The Government Printing Office sold all its copies within a day. Paperback editions were rushed into print. The transcripts were even read on television. The good will created by the president's speech didn't last long.

The heavily edited transcripts were often vague. As a case against Richard Nixon, they contained little hard evidence. But the tone of the conversations was clear. The Nixon White House was much as John Dean had described it. The tapes showed a White House in which Nixon and his aides were eager to get things done but rarely interested in right and wrong. Also, many of the conversations contained foul language, which had been replaced with the words "expletive deleted." Republican Senator Hugh Scott summed up the reaction of many who read the transcripts. He called the conversations a "deplorable, disgusting, shabby, immoral performance."

Both Congress and Jaworski vowed to press for the actual tapes. A week later, several newspapers began to call for the president's resignation.

On May 20, Judge Sirica granted Jaworski's subpoena of sixty-four tapes. When the president's lawyers appealed the decision, Jaworski decided to take an unusual step. He asked that the case go directly to the Supreme Court to avoid delay. The Court agreed to hear the case, but not for several months.

The White House decided to show that the president had more important duties than the Watergate investigations. Since his trip to China, Nixon's foreign policy had been the most successful part of his presidency. Nixon decided to make a pair of diplomatic journeys.

The first was to the Middle East. Enthusiastic crowds greeted the president in Egypt. Nixon flew on to Syria and finished the tour in Israel.

After only a few days at home, the

The April 11, 1974, House Judiciary Committee subpoena that ordered Nixon to turn over forty-two tapes.

ORIGINAL

BY AUTHORITY OF THE HOUSE OF REPRESENTATIVES OF THE CONGRESS OF THE UNITED STATES OF AMERICA

To Benjamin Marshall, or his duly authorized representative:

You are hereby commanded to summon

Richard M. Nixon, President of the United States of America, or any subordinate officer, official or employee with custody or control of the things described in the attached schedule,

to be and appear before the Committee on the Judiciary

Committee of the House of Representatives of the United States, of which the Hon.

Peter W. Rodino, Jr. is chairman, and to bring with him the things specified in the schedule attached hereto and made a part hereof,

in their chamber in the city of Washington, on or before April 25, 1974, at the hour of 10:00 A.M. then and there to produce and deliver said things to said Committee, or their duly authorized representative, in connection with the Committee's investigation authorized and directed by H. Res. 803, adopted February 6, 1974.

Herein fail not, and make return of this summons.

Witness my hand and the seal of the House of Representatives of the United States, at the city of Washington, this 11th day of April, 1974.

Peter W. Rodino, Jr.   Chairman.

Attest:

_____
Clerk

Leonid Brezhnev, leader of the Soviet Union, and President Nixon, during Nixon's trip to the Soviet Union in June 1974.

A record of the House Judiciary Committee's vote to adopt articles of impeachment against President Nixon

president left the country again. He traveled to the Soviet Union to meet with that country's leader, Leonid Brezhnev.

Back at home, the foreign visits were overshadowed by the Watergate. Some people believed the president was trying to distract the nation from the scandal. They called Nixon's trips "Watergate diplomacy."

On July 24, Nixon lost his last court case for the tapes. The Supreme Court unanimously ruled in *United States* v. *Richard M. Nixon* that the White House had to supply the subpoenaed tapes. This ruling by the nation's highest court ended President Nixon's claim of executive privilege.

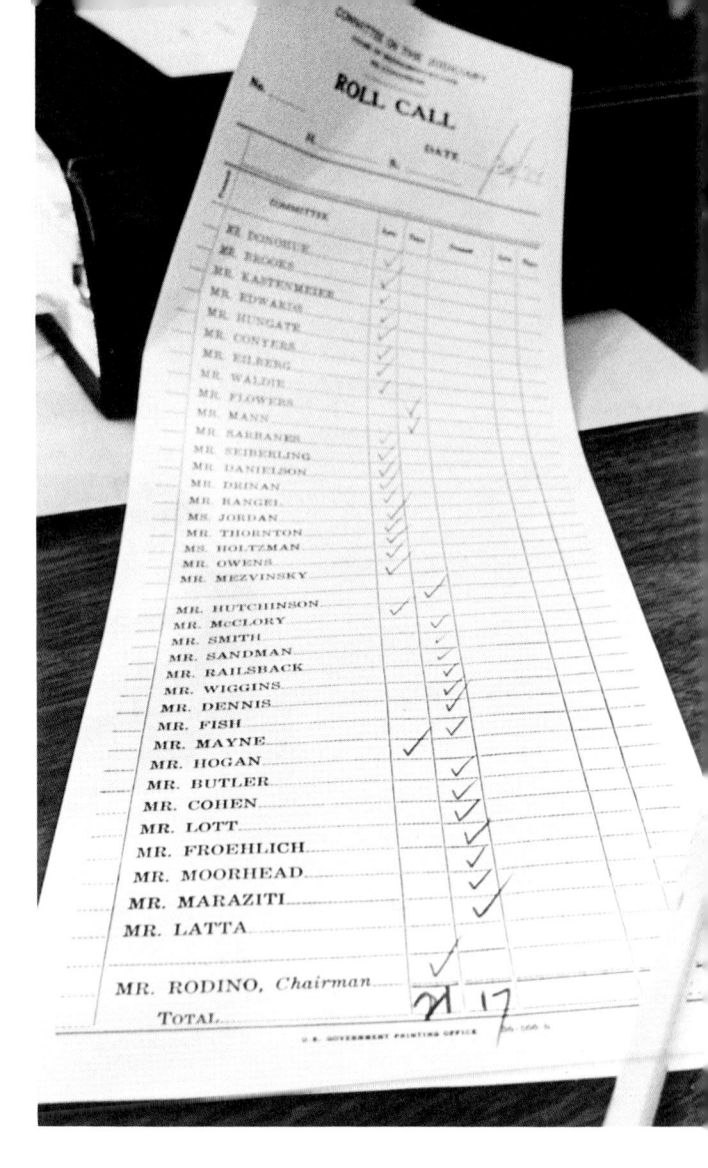

Three days later, on July 27, the House Judiciary Committee passed its first article of impeachment. This article centered on Nixon's obstruction of justice. It mentioned the Watergate break-in and Nixon's use of presidential power to halt the investigations. It charged that Nixon had "prevented, obstructed, and impeded the administration of justice." This was in "violation of his con-

54

Members of the National Citizens Committee for Fairness to the Presidency march in support of Richard Nixon on May 9, 1974.

stitutional duty to take care that the laws be faithfully executed." Millions of people watched on television as the committee voted. There were twenty-seven votes for the first article of impeachment, eleven against.

The committee passed two more articles of impeachment. The second article also dealt with Nixon's misuse of his authority. He was accused of conduct "violating the constitutional rights of citizens." By ordering the FBI and Secret Service to spy on American citizens, the article charged, Nixon had broken his oath to uphold the law. It also charged him with maintaining a secret White House investigative unit with its unlawful use of the CIA. The last article charged Nixon with refusing to obey Congress's subpoenas. Thus the committee, by voting for these three articles, recommended that members of the House of Representatives vote on impeachment.

The approaching impeachment vote against Nixon meant that he would then have to stand trial before the Senate of the United States. If two-thirds of the Senate voted against Nixon, he would be removed from office.

Pressure was mounting on Nixon from other areas, too. A congressional committee had discovered that the president had paid only $1,000 in federal

55

President Nixon during his resignation speech of August 8, 1974.

taxes in 1971 and 1972, while earning the presidential salary of $200,000 per year. Critics also questioned the millions of government dollars Nixon had spent on his houses in Key Biscayne, Florida, and San Clemente, California. The White House claimed the money—amounting to more than $10 million—was used to provide "security" for the president and his family. Others believed the spending had been unnecessary and wasteful. And there was the question of Nixon's 1969 "gift" to the National Archives. Nixon had given his vice-presidential papers to the institution, but he had deducted what he believed was half their worth—$235,000—from his taxes. Each new scandal led to more calls for Nixon's impeachment.

Just as he had after the 1960 election, Nixon had to make a decision weighing his own wishes against the good of the country. The Senate trial would last for weeks or months. The normal business of government would halt as the impeachment process consumed Congress and the president. On the other hand, Nixon felt that he couldn't just walk away from the presidency—a goal he had worked long and hard to achieve. To those around him, President Nixon seemed tortured by indecision. He directed his lawyers to begin preparing a defense.

On August 5, the White House quietly released an overdue transcript of the tapes. Nixon's staff warned supporters that the public reaction to the tapes' contents might be bad.

The transcribed recording was from June 23, 1972, only a week after the break-in. In the transcript, Nixon specifically ordered Haldeman to tell the CIA to halt the FBI's investigation of Watergate. Until now, many people had thought that Nixon was innocent—that only the people who served him had committed crimes. The new tape made it clear: Nixon was personally involved in the cover-up, almost from the start.

The tape was devastating. It now seemed impossible that the president could win his trial in the Senate. When the White House announced that the president would address the country on the night of August 8, few doubted what he would say.

At nine o'clock, Richard Nixon made his last speech as president. He spoke

Accompanied by Gerald Ford and his wife Betty, Richard and Pat Nixon prepare to leave the White House following Nixon's resignation.

of his accomplishments rather than his mistakes. He admitted only that he had lost the support of Congress, which he needed to govern the nation. He said, "I have never been a quitter. To leave office before my term is complete is abhorrent to every instinct in my body. But, as president, I must put the interests of America first. America needs a full-time president and a full-time Congress. Therefore, I shall resign the presidency effective at noon tomorrow."

The next day, Secretary of State Henry Kissinger received a letter. It read,

Dear Mr. Secretary,
    I hereby resign the Office of President of the United States.
                  Richard Nixon

That morning, the president addressed a tearful White House staff. Then he boarded a helicopter and began a journey back to his home in San Clemente, California.

At noon the vice president, Gerald R. Ford, took the oath of office. Ford became the thirty-seventh president of the United States. In his first speech to the American people, he said, "Our long national nightmare is over."

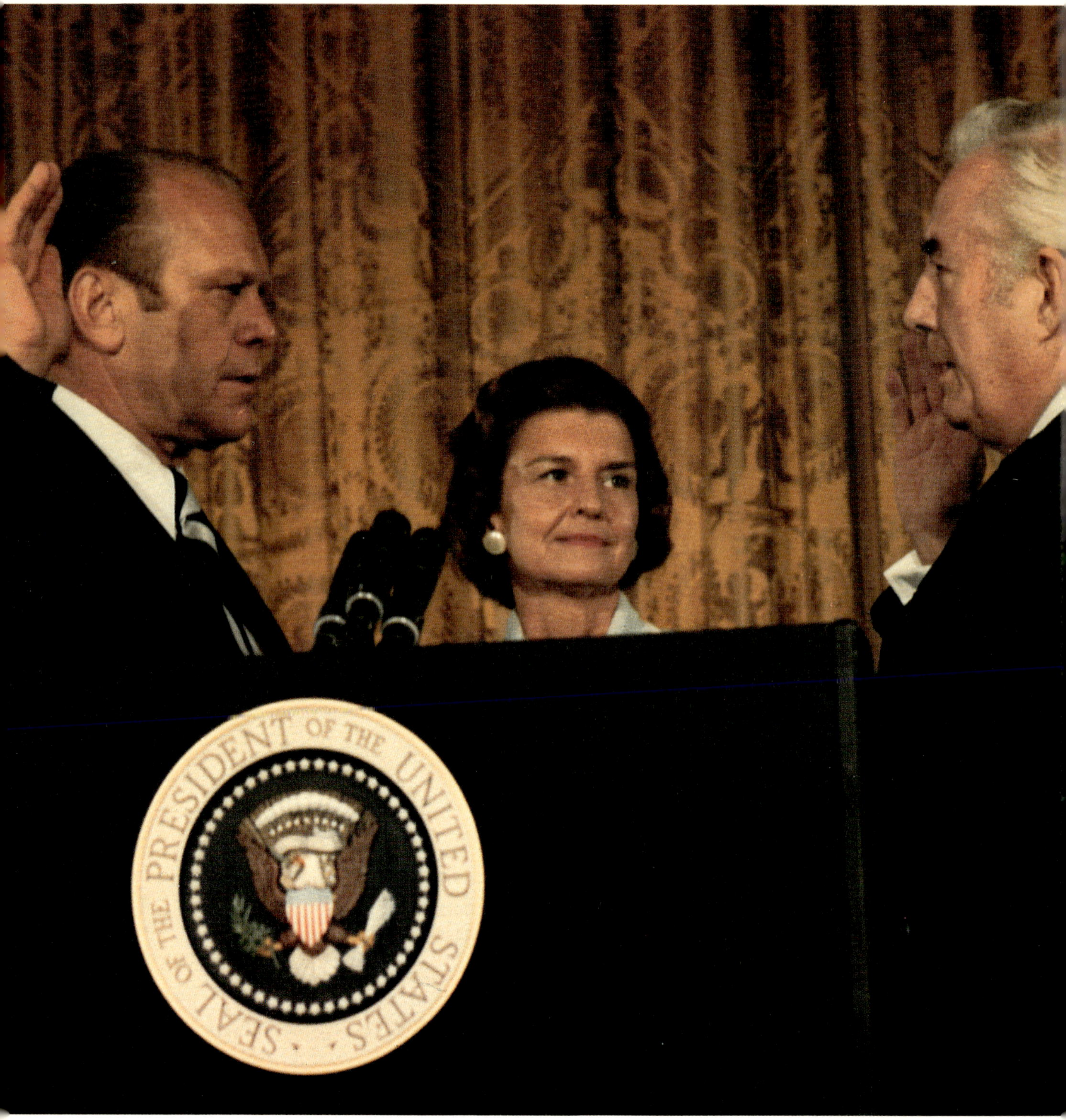
SEAL OF THE PRESIDENT OF THE UNITED STATES

AFTERWORD

A TIME OF HEALING

On August 9, 1974, Gerald R. Ford became the first president of the United States who had never won a national election. Vice President Spiro T. Agnew had resigned on October 10, 1973, after a scandal of his own. Ford had been appointed as vice president by Nixon, and both houses of Congress approved the appointment. Ford had only been vice president for eight months when Nixon resigned.

Ford quickly tried to restore the tarnished image of the presidency. Nixon wasn't invited to Ford's swearing-in ceremony. Soon after taking office, Ford replaced much of Nixon's staff. Of Nixon's most important advisers, only Henry Kissinger remained. Ford urged "a time of healing" and vowed to work with the mostly Democratic Congress to solve the nation's problems.

A month after Nixon's departure, Ford pardoned the former president for all crimes he might have committed in office. Many Americans, still angry at the pain caused by Watergate, felt that Ford's action was wrong. The pardon meant that Nixon could never be brought to trial for his part in the Watergate affair. They thought that Ford had possibly promised Nixon a pardon in exchange for his nomination as vice president—something that Ford strongly denied. Other people, however, believed Ford had acted wisely. The sight of a former president on trial or in prison, they felt, would have damaged the United States's image to the rest of the world.

The trials of the other Watergate conspirators continued, however. In all, over seventy people were indicted in Watergate-related crimes. Many of Nixon's closest aides, including Haldeman, Ehrlichman, and Mitchell, went to jail for crimes such as perjury, obstruction of justice, and conspiracy. The men served from one to four years in prison each. Nixon's accuser, John Dean, also was imprisoned for conspiracies com-

Gerald Ford is officially sworn in as president.

President Ford announcing his pardon of Richard Nixon.

mitted at the White House. Most of those indicted or convicted never went to prison, however. In one of the last legal actions of Watergate, Richard Nixon lost his right to practice law in New York.

For two years, the nation had watched the spectacle of Watergate. In that time, other problems had arisen. The new president faced a growing economic crisis. Prices were rising, and unemployment was higher than at any time since the Great Depression. In the 1974 congressional elections, anger at the state of the economy and Ford's pardon of Nixon hurt Republican candidates. These elections were the first since Nixon's resignation. The Democrats greatly increased their majorities in both houses of Congress. Two years later, Ford lost the presidency to Democratic candidate Jimmy Carter.

The Watergate Hotel, where the burglars were arrested, gave its name to an era as well as a single scandal. The crisis reshaped the way Americans view their government. The tapes were an unforgettable lesson in the grim realities of politics. They showed that a man with a historic vision of peace could also be terribly flawed.

At the center of Watergate was one question: Is the president above the law? The scandal gives important insight into our form of government. The power that we entrust to the president must be limited by the higher power of the Constitution.

The Watergate scandal tested the rule of law. The crisis pitted the power of the presidency against that of the legislative and judicial branches. Nixon's actions threatened the separation of powers, which is at the heart of the Constitution. Finally, however, the checks and balances of the system held the nation together. Through the actions of the courts, the Congress, and finally the president himself, the Constitution was preserved.

The scandal, and the way it ended, is proof that the United States has a government of laws, not of men.

An anti-Nixon poster shows many of those arrested in connection with Watergate—but notes that Richard Nixon remains free.

WANTED

JAMES McCORD	DWIGHT CHAPIN	H.R. HALDEMAN	JOHN MITCHELL	JOHN ERLICHMAN
MAURICE STANS	EUGENIO MARTINEZ	G. GORDON LIDDY	CHARLES COLSON	HERBERT KALMBACH
JOHN DEAN	ROBERT MARDIAN	JEB MAGRUDER	RICHARD M. NIXON	BERNARD L. BARKER
VIRGILIO GONZALEZ	DONALD SEGRETTI	FRANK A. STURGIS	E. HOWARD HUNT JR.	HUGH SLOAN JR.

APPREHENDED

INDEX

Page numbers in *italics* indicate illustrations

Agnew, Spiro, 19, 46, 47, *47*
antiwar protest, 19, 23

Baker, Howard H., 37, 40-41, 43
Barker, Bernard L., 27, 31
Belsen, James A., 7
Bernstein, Carl, 28
Bork, Robert H., 48
Brezhnev, Leonid, 21, 54, *54*
Brown, Pat, 16
Budget and Impoundment Control Act, 50
Burger, Warren, *34*
Butterfield, Alexander, 43
Byrne, Mathew, 40

Cambodia, 23
Carter, Jimmy, 60
Castro, Fidel, 31
Central Intelligence Agency (CIA), 29, 31, 56
Chambers, Whittaker, *13*, 14
Checkers speech, 14, 15, 40
China, 16, 20, 20-21
cold war, 13, 16-17
Committee on Banking and Currency, 28
Committee to Re-elect the President (CRP), 8, 26, 28, 29, 38
communism, fear of, 12-13, 15
Constitution, 38, 47, 50, 51, 60
Cox, Archibald, 40, 45, 46, 48, 49

Dahlberg, Kenneth H., 28
Dash, Samuel, 40
Dean, John W. III, 25, 29, 31, 35, 38, 39, 40-43, *42*, 52, 59
testimony of, 40-43, *42*
Democratic National Committee, break-in at, 7-9, *8*
Democratic National Convention, 18
détente, 21
dirty tricks, played at, 31

Dole, Robert, 32
Douglas, Helen Gahagan, 15

Ehrlichman, John, 20, 25, 39, 40, 46, 50, 59
18-minute gap, 49-50
Eisenhower, Dwight D., 15
Ellsberg, Daniel, 23, 39, 40
enemies list, 42
Ervin, Samuel, 35, 36, 37, *37*
executive privilege, 38, 51, 53

Federal Bureau of Investigation (FBI), 23, 27, 28, 35, 55, 56
Fifth Amendment, 38
Ford, Gerald, 46, 57, *57*, 58
and Nixon pardon, 59, 60

General Accounting Office, 28, 29
Gonzalez, Virgilio R., 31
grand jury, 27
Gray, L. Patrick, 27, 29, 35, 38
Great Society, 17

Haiphong, 35
Haldeman, H. R. (Robert), 20, 25, 29, 39, *39*, 51, 59
Hanoi, 35
Hiss, Alger, 13-14, 32
Hoover, J. Edgar, 23
House Un-American Activities Committee, 13
Humphrey, Hubert, *18*, 20
Hunt, E. Howard, 8, *24*, 25, 26, 27, 28, 29, 31, 36, 38-39, *39*, *46*
Huston, Tom C., 23

immunity, 38
impeachment, 47-48, 50, 52, 54
impoundment, 50-51

Jaworski, Leon, *48*, 49, 51, 52
Johnson, Andrew, 49
Johnson, Lyndon B., 17, 18, *18*
Judiciary Committee, 51, 54

Justice Department, 28, 29, 31, 48, 57

Kalmbach, Herbert W., 31
Kennedy, Edward, 33, 35
Kennedy, John F., 16, 17
Kennedy, Robert, 18
Khrushchev, Nikita, 15-16
Kissinger, Henry, 20, 21, 23, 57, 59
Kitchen Debate, 16
Kleindienst, Richard G., 29, 39

Latin America, 15
Liddy, G. Gordon, *24*, 27, *28*, 29, 31, 36, 38-39

McCarthy, Joseph, 15
McCord, James W., Jr., 7-8, 26, *26*, 31, 36-37, 38, 40
McGovern, George, 7, 23, 32
Magruder, Jeb, 40
Mao Zedong, *20*
Martinez, Eugenio R., 31
Middle East, 52
Mitchell, John N., 20, 23, 25, 27, 29, 40, *46*, 51, 59

National Archives, 56
New York Post, 38
New York Times, 23, 27
Nixon, Pat (Ryan), *10*, 11, *34*, 57
Nixon, Richard Milhous
advisers of, 20
and Agnew, 47
anti-communism of, 11-13, 15
background of, 11, 12
Checkers speech, 14, 15, 40
in China, 20, 20-21
and Congress, 21
in Congressional campaigns, 13, 15
election of 1960, 16
election of 1968, 18-20, *19*
election of 1972, 30, 31-32, 33
financial scandals of, 15, 55-56

62

   in Hiss investigation, *13*, 13-14, 32
   and impeachment, 47-48, 48, 54-55
   pardon of, 59, 60
   and press, 32-33
   resignation of, 44, *55*, 56-57
   in Soviet Union, 15-16, 21, 53-54
   and subpoenaed tapes, 45, 51, 52, 54
   as unindicted co-conspirator, 51
   as vice president, 14, 15-16
   and Vietnam War, 19, 21, 23, 35, 50
   and Watergate diplomacy, 54
   and Watergate scandal, 30, 38, 39-40, 41, 43, 55

O'Brien, Lawrence F., 27

Pentagon Papers, 23, 39
plumbers, 42
presidential power
   executive privilege, 38, 51, 53
   impeachment and, 48-49, 54-55
   limits on, 49-51
pumpkin papers, 14

Republican National Convention, 19, 30
Richardson, Elliot, 48
Richney, Charles, 30
Rodino, Peter, 51
Ruckelshaus, William D., 48

Saturday Night Massacre, 48
Scott, Hugh, 52
Segretti, Donald H., 31
Senate Watergate Committee, 35, 36, *37*, 37-38, 39, 40-43, 42, 45
separation of powers, 38, 51, 60
Silbert, Earl, 27, 29
silent majority, 19
Sirica, John J., 29, *30*, 36, 37, 46, 52
Six Crises (Nixon), 16
Soviet Union, 12, 13, 21, 54
special prosecutor, 40, 45, 46, 47
Stalin, Joseph, 12
Stennis, John C., 47-48
Sturgis, Frank A., 31, 38
subpoena, 31, 38, 53
   of White House tapes, 45
Supreme Court, 52, 54
surveillance devices, 23, 31, 32

Time magazine, 31
Twenty-fifth Amendment, 47

United States v. *Richard M. Nixon*, 54

Vesco, Robert, 28
Vietnamization, 23
Vietnam War, 17-18, 21, 22, 23, 35, 50
Voorhis, Jerry, 13

Wallace, George C., 18
War Powers Act, 50

Washington Post, 26, 31, 32
Watergate complex, 6, 7
Watergate diplomacy, 54
Watergate scandal and burglars' trial, 27, 29, 30, 31, 36-37
   burglary of Democratic National Committee, 7-9, 8
   burglary of Ellsberg's psychiatrist's office, 38-39
   cover-up, 25-26, 29-30
   dirty tricks in, 31-32, *32*
   impact of, 60
   indictment of Nixon aides, 51, 59-60, 61
   investigations of, 26-29, 33
   Nixon and, 30, 38, 39-40, 41, 43, 55
   resignation of Nixon aides, 39
   Senate Committee, 35, 36, 37, 37-38, 39, 40-43, 42, 45
   and special prosecutor, 40, 45, 46-47
   subpoena of White House tapes, 43, 45-46, 48-49, 50, 51, 52, 54
White House tapes, 43, 45-46, 48-49, 50, 51, 52, 54
Whittier, California, 11
Wills, Frank, 7
wiretaps. *See* surveillance devices
Woods, Rose Mary, 7, 50, *50*
Woodward, Bob, 26-27

Ziegler, Ronald, 8

SUGGESTED READING

Ambrose, Stephen E. *Nixon: The Education of a Politician, 1913–1962.* New York: Simon & Schuster, 1988.

Archer, Jules. *Watergate: America in Crisis.* New York: Thomas Y. Crowell, 1974.

Bernstein, Carl, and Bob Woodward. *All The President's Men.* New York: Simon & Schuster, 1974.

———. *The Final Days.* New York: Simon & Schuster, 1987.

Hargrove, Jim. *Richard M. Nixon: The Thirty-Seventh President.* Chicago: Childrens Press, 1985.

Jaworski, Leon. *The Right and the Power: The Prosecution of Watergate.* Houston: Gulf Publishing, 1976.

The Nixon-Ford Years (Political Profiles Series). New York: Facts on File, 1982.

Nixon, Richard. *In the Arena: A Memoir of Victory, Defeat, and Renewal.* New York: Simon & Schuster, 1990.

Ripley, C. Peter. *Richard Nixon.* New York: Chelsea House, 1987.

The Washington Post Staff. *The Fall of the President.* New York: Dell, 1976.

Picture Credits

Gerald R. Ford Library: 58, 60.
Library of Congress: 61.
Lyndon B. Johnson Library: 18.
NASA: 21.
National Archives: 17, 20, 32, 34, 36, 41, 57.
U.S. Army: 22.
UPI/Bettmann Newsphotos: 49.
Wide World Photos: 6, 8, 10, 12, 13, 14, 19, 25, 26, 27, 28, 30, 37, 39, 42, 45, 46, 47, 49, 50, 51, 53, 54 (both), 55, 56, 57.

About the Author

Scott Westerfeld designs educational software and interactive videos and lives in New York City. He has taught high school, has edited textbooks, and is also the author of *The Berlin Airlift* in the *Turning Points in American History* series.

WOODBRIDGE/ELEMENTARY
SCHOOL LIBRARY
ZEELAND PUBLIC SCHOOLS